Shelf Life

For Baylor
6/17/1949 — 9/24/2001

For Ann,
for the love of words.
— Elizabeth

Shelf Life

ISBN: 978-0-578-47883-8

Copyright © 2019 Elizabeth E. Landrum

Printed in the United States of America

Peapod Studio
Lopez Island, Washington

Ingram Spark Press

I prefer the skyline

of a shelf of books.

Treasure is what you find

Already in your pocket, friend.

Ted Kooser and Jim Harrison,
"Braided Creek: a conversation in poetry"

The poems in this collection were inspired by discoveries made while dusting a bookcase. Photographs were taken and altered by the author, using photophunia.com sketch effects.

Memories

Roots

What Goes On

Memories

What We Save and What Saves Us

Start with an inventory of my bookcase
— each object dusted with mystery,
each its own suitcase packed with light.
If it had been the other way,
if you were the one left behind to sort,
you would have puzzled over
these yellowed recipes, arrays of stones,
feathers, a lock of hair, matchbooks, hats,
buttons, beads, antlers — strange to a stranger.

Grease-stained, dog-eared, and tattered
The Joy of Cooking 1958 edition, barely bound
with rubber bands, remembers the time
our mother's Thanksgiving turkey tumbled
out of the oven, onto the floor
as the rest of the family arrived —
one more course in recomposure and grace,
the only ways she knew to save the day.

One braided leather riding crop, bone-handled,
silver-collared, stands sentry guarding a memory —
the day when riding with our Great Uncle Wallis,
I somersaulted over the horse's neck, clutching
then releasing her mane, and stifling my tears
until it felt safe to remount, as our uncle
whispered secrets in her ear.

That grey felt fedora, with its flat bow and
red feather accent, reminds me how Dad
continued to work through all of the changes
after polio struck – wheelchair, to crutches,
to brace, then his own weak legs to carry him,
and always, always the hat.

Curious how objects can awaken the dead
and me from my usual sleep,
how when I let them fall open, I rise
to my latest occasion.
If it had been the other way, this shelf
would contain no fishing hat, no prayer beads,

no six-pound rock – luminous, blue,
jagged as the cut of its Yellowstone River
where you asked us to scatter your ashes,
knowing those five days we rode on horses
to your sacred refuge would offer a taste
of your wilderness, your wildness, and
your lasting lesson: *Say Yes to Life.*

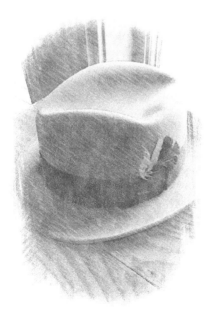

The Archaeology of Dusting

We do not know until the shell breaks what kind of egg we have been sitting on
— T.S. Eliot

i

Dusting a bookcase is nothing like
quick slips of cloth across baseboards,
windowsills and toilet tops.
Try slowing the dance
to notice the mysteries,
histories, poetry and art —
artifacts begging for excavation
like eggs you've been sitting on,
shells ready to break.

ii.

Not ashamed to say I stayed all day to
re-read grandmother's memoir, her voice
clear and present with notions foreign, yet
familiar. We settled in our easy chairs,
her cheeks aglow in gaslight, mine whitened
by LED, shared tea and talk of propriety,
politics, and family while I took notes
for my future memoir.

iii.

A clay teapot jostled as my hand
reached for the microscopic detritus.
It nodded approval, then spouted
questions about its origin, form and
finish, so I traded the cloth for a
pencil to trace the unusual shape,
research its history for answers
to calm its unsettled position.

iv.

Uncovering grandfather's papers
led to a deeper fall —
weeks down a rabbit hole, chasing
archived letters and clippings,
a trove of invitations into a den
of Appalachian culture, violent times
between world wars and tales of a man
I believed I knew —
discoveries, like dust, ever-building.

v.

Easy to understand how Alice felt.
Too tall for the door, too small
to reach the key, then to encounter
a caterpillar asking
Who Are You?
when you've already changed
several times since morning.

Ode to an Unglazed Teapot

Red
Bisque-fired
There is not a way in, and
no way out — a window in
the middle framed agape
Triangle topping the lid like a belfry
Straight vertical lines and a sharp
angled spout that could never
pour tea   No handle
to raise   the weight
too great   It speaks
of ceremony, patience, and
traces of promise. I haven't
washed my hand of the wet
earth's sweet memory. I, too
have been hardened by fire,
tempered to endure the rain.

Over seven years ago in a ceramics studio I witnessed how a glaze fire can transform art or condemn someone's treasures to the shard pile outside, and it was there that I measured and cut the 18 tarpaper patterns, rolled each damp slab to an exact 7/16th, sliced and sized the pieces, beveling their edges with an x-acto knife, then arranged each shape on a porous board to dry to a perfect leather-hardness for a slurry to fuse them together so they could stand for the slow low fire, and return to me unharmed, still too new-born to commit to a glaze, still afraid to surrender to one more indifferent fire.

Memory

Maybe its strands exist in woven bracelets
like ones we made from dandelion chains
in the yellow meadow of our childhood
when we learned we could disperse
hundreds of feathery seeds
with just a single sigh —
threads untangled
and tumbled
in time

Maybe there is no end to the rising of
moments that sharpen themselves
on unexpected openings of links
and files, or to the seductive
strangeness that suspends
just before the word
you were seeking
emerges clear
untainted by
waiting

Conversations Unremembered

These empty bowls rest undisturbed,
napkins rolled and ringed,
forks aligned.

Someone jerked the tablecloth —
wine-stained and long-ago discarded.
All of the candles stand hollow.

This polished wood reflects
vacant eyes too blind by time
to piece it back together.

There were six. I sat at the end.
It was pasta we ate from these bowls,
our words that ghosts consumed.

I remember the laughter — hardy,
tumbling like waterfalls over a cliff,
but there are clocks I can't reverse

like that video clip where water falls
up, and a man becomes a boy,
conversations garbled.

My current companions are
uncertainties that play like children,
pulling from trunks in an attic

treasures that confuse them or
look like someone else's junk.
Maybe I'll welcome the questions

that burn as they circle. It is the
asking that returns me to myself
each time I set this table.

He Was the Race Car & I Was the Scottie Dog

It was as endless as it seemed
in the Hall of Mirrors, as thrilling
as the tilt of the ferris wheel —
all cotton candy, corndogs and carousels,
and mine for the taking, like the giant panda
I won by a lucky toss of the ring.
The grownups said it was rigged —
Don't waste your nickels
but my brother prodded me to try.

He stood there beside me, squeezed
my hand the first time I stepped up
to the rollercoaster platform, and he
taught me how to drive a bumper car
so he could plow into mine with no regret.

At home, he insisted I play Monopoly
even when I voted for Clue, and he always
seemed to own the hotels, the orange
and the red streets where I had to pay rent.
But then I would need him
to let me out of jail for free, and he would
make me a loan to keep the game going.
I thought it would always be like that.

One Knee Down In the River

Dust has claimed the frame of your picture.
I blow it away, stroke the wood, sniff the glass.
There, in your felt hat and blue waders,
one knee down in the River called Hope,
you gleam as you offer that trout to the camera.
Dripping, slick and glistening, a fish exhausted,
outsmarted in your last cast and struggle, lies
cradled, fins between your fingers, moments
before the release.

Today I pretend we are together
so I can ask you about those times we shouted
Hi Ho Silver! before racing our bikes downhill,
heedless of potholes, wind in our eyes.
Did you ever let me win? And just how did
we sneak out of that third story window,
escaping to chase more shooting stars?
Who were we then? You, my Clyde Barrow,
my Lone Ranger. And who was I to you?

I want to read you my poetry, listen
to your edits, show you my home.
I want to hear you sing again — every word
of *Alice's Restaurant* and *Desolation Row*
like you did that night in Noni's barn. But
layers of time have turned your voice thin
and gauzy, transcribed our stories
in fading ink, exchanged image
after image for air.

I want to tell you about Dad's dying,
how he asked only for peace, quiet, water.
Then permission to go. I want to know how
it was for you, your last cast and struggle
when you tried to climb the stairs, crumpled
to your knees. When you insisted I bring you the
crossword puzzle, your Sunday ritual, and you
strained to stay with it, nodding, pen in hand,
just before you were jerked from the stream.

Sometimes in dreams we talk.
Sometimes you are a river unfinished,
a fly rod, a cobweb, a fly,
a brown trout disguised in the silt.
But this is not a dream of silence.
It's a shuffling of papers sealed
in the ceiling. It's a clawing at the hatch.
Please smuggle me in
before the ladder collapses.

Rediscovering Slovenly Peter

Perhaps it is only in childhood that books have any deep influence on our lives.
— Graham Green
Keep fear out of your child's mind, as you would keep poison out of his body;
for fear is the deadliest of mental poisons.   — Orison Swett Marden

Choose one broken spine, tattered cover,
a friendless boy sporting tangled hair,
fingernails corkscrewed and dangling.
Awaken inside this children's book of
"happy tales and funny pictures" — See
Johnny plummet off the end of a wharf
only because he wants to know
how swallows fly, his nose to the sky.
See how the fish are mocking?

Watch chubby Augustus refuse his soup
then fade away, a mere four days to his grave.
Open wide your eyes as orange flames are
claiming Pauline's apron, chasing up her spine,
swirling her braids. See how quick she changes
into a mound of ash.
Watch how her horrified kittens mourn.

Turn the page to a day that Little Crybaby
cannot seem to be cheerful. She snivels until
her eyes tumble out of their sockets. See her
eyeballs there at her feet, fixed in a stare?
See her lost and blind, stomping the ground,
hands flailing. Then look at the blood,
bright as it drips, thick as it pools,
around Conrad's severed thumbs.
See how the tailor dances with his
nine foot shears, and delights in the plight
of one more thumb-sucking child.

Let your tongue dance and
taste the sound of every clever couplet.
Don't swallow. See if you can breathe.
Let the mind release as you
count the beats of each slow line
instead of your quickening pulse.
Then try to forget the pictures.

Can you dismiss even one sadistic image
that's meant to inhibit each time you
strike a match, observe a bird overhead, or
decline a serving of soup?
Next time you raise a hand to your mouth,
simply resist the stench of blood.
It's just your imagination at play.

Try not to think of that poor blind girl
when you must cry your eyes out too.
See if you can weep somewhere other than
the shower. You might need a hacksaw
to crack the shackles of habits
grown from little fictions of fright.

Everything Changes

I scan Get Well notes that arrive
beside the sympathy cards.
Some other me watches
as I choose what to save —
one gray felt fedora
in a box labeled "good hat",
pocket knife, shoeshine brush,
his last appointment book,
a tan cashmere scarf and
plaid flannel shirt I'll wear home,
returning, but not quite.

Everything changes,
and yet we go on, pace through
days as if rehearsed —
fill baskets with his chosen foods,
fold handkerchiefs into tidy squares,
place them in their dresser drawer,
retrieve his starched dress shirts
from the dry cleaners while silent,
disguised, surprised by everything
that looks unchanged.

In a moment charged and ripe
with revelations, stunned we sip
and thirst for more. How swiftly
the hollowness enters.
How we strain to swallow the mystery.

The instant when everything
changes, a memory
engraves itself. Dad watched
as I took my first breath.
I watched as he took his last.
He listened for something beyond,
mumbled *OK. Let's Go!*
Then he did.

14

Learning to Listen

Silence is not the absence of something but the presence of everything.
— Gordon Hempton

Once I retreated for silence,
invested half a day in listening
to a waterfall, eyes shut, hands cupped
behind my ears to tease out the piccolos,
flutes, the blue notes riffing behind,
the other half spent on the edge
of a creek to worship with stones
while they made their joyful noise.
I could even hear their closing song,
the jeweled jazz of a purpling sky.

Then daybreak. Alone on a beach
I lounged until noon, shoulders cradled
inside a drift log,
its ancient wood the perfect diaphragm
to amplify every call and response
like kettle drums in my bones.
Salt tears sang back to the sea.

A true recluse would need
no other kind of conversation,
no explanation for the absence
of loneliness, no word for hurt, but I
hurried away in search of a phone,
so I could recount the concerts, and
a pen for my trowel to unearth a phrase.
My tongue dried like cotton
and I could excavate only air.

Everyday Delusion

My dog killed a deer today.
I heard the bleating in the woods.
There was no blood. Tears fogged
my vision as the doe kicked the air
to get away, flailed and flopped
like a fish worn down by the strength
of a fisherman's line, then withered,
downed by a creature more fervent
and determined — the one that held
in his bones a blueprint for this victory.
My dog killed a deer today.
He knew I would not approve, yet
his head swelled with adrenaline
and with pride.

My dog killed a deer today.
I thought about last night when I kissed
his downy crown, tucked him in, told
him what a good and gentle boy he is.
I thought about how I soothe myself
with stories that obscure his nature
and mine, believing he wants nothing
more than love,
and I could never kill for sport.

Sophie's Moment

It was that moment she suddenly
sprinted toward the sea.
There was nothing but Sophie
and her ocean,
the rest of the world at her back.

Green ruffles finned in the wind.
Little pink soles pounded
on damp sand, but
her thirty pounds, all power
and pluck, left no prints,
and the camera's click
could not quite capture
the swell and surge of pure rapture.

Her tiny hands raised high,
as if to praise the coming tide,
with fathoms of delight,
she cried, "Stop waves! Stop!"
and when they did not comply,
she scampered faster, just in case
they couldn't hear her order
above the roll and crash of their answer.

It was that moment to save,
to frame a memory of innocence
before the rupture and tumble,
before we glimpsed our impotence,
before we learned to be afraid.

Roots

For the Ghosts of my Ancestors

If the ways of my kin were written,
rituals laid down to read
like bedtime stories
over and over again until
I could dream their dreams,
absorb them into my bones,

if photographs fading in albums
could speak their names
in each unique voice
and ghosts could return
to tell their versions of the stories
I've heard and others I haven't, and

if the shadows that circle their brows
could clear for just one moment,
awaken a musical strain or release a
certain scent that could lead me
down some well-trodden trail

then maybe I could glimpse the shape
of their hearts, bury them in my chest,
carry them through the alleyways
of my most difficult days.
And yet I would still not know

which particles of my body belong
to which members of my tribe, or
the roles they are playing
in my current performance

and surely each answer
would become another question,
another answer
locked in the vault.

Not Out of the Realm

My parents met in a cyclone.
She let down her hair. He climbed up.
All night a magic harp played music
as they shared their golden egg. Soon
winged monkeys were summoned
to lead them on to the emerald city.

And I was born in a manger.
It was no more miracle
than any other birth.
The donkeys brayed
like my mother did
when I plopped on the hay.

My brothers were frogs
who had to work hard
to earn their crowns,
while the princes I kissed
offered only a too-tight shoe.
The day I saw the emperor strut
in his naked regalia, I realized
the sky was not falling.

a Friday in September, 1955 Louisville, Kentucky

Back then I loved Fridays, those mornings
my mother returned from the bus stop
with Georgia in the red Chevy wagon's back seat
where Georgia insisted on sitting.

There was comfort in the rhythm of her hips
while she ironed my daddy's white shirts, polished
the silver, mopped and vacuumed our floors,
and it was the gospel tunes she hummed
that lingered in every room until the next Friday.

Georgia's hugs were somehow wider than
her arms, and when she laughed, it lasted all day.
She called my mamma *Maaaam*,
my brother *You Rascal*, and me, well,
I was *Sweetie*, and I believed I was the only one.
I didn't know she worked in five other houses.

And I never pictured her family, or her home,
its back porch sagging
under the weight of laundry baskets ---
more clothes to iron, after the bus ride back.
I never saw her as a great granddaughter
of slaves, or myself as descended from people
who owned people.

These things just weren't discussed.
And I never heard *the N word* spoken
until first grade where my friends were
easy with words they'd heard.

Then there was that Friday
after school.
I said the word full.
Georgie kept on ironing.
I might have seen her wince,
but she just said
Oh Sweetie, that's not a nice word.

Later, I apologized.
Much later grappled with the hurt.
Today as I write this, I can't ignore
my contortions as I try to pretend
that naming it by a single letter
might unfasten it from its shackles,
conceal the scars, mop up the blood.

"No one has to read my silly musings"
(a found poem taken from *Family Affairs by May*,
grandmother's memoir)

One strict rule   my mother had
never discuss   family affairs
outside the home   perhaps it's this repression
that gives me the urge   I shall do it
on paper   no one has to read

Unless you have lived   where muddy waters surround your house
you will never know the peace you feel when you live high
high on a mountainside   the world would be a better place if
everyone lived in a small town no real ghettos and plenty of clean air

We were ardent drys   when you serve nothing alcoholic
you have to feature eating   the success in an old ham is in the cooking
everything was done with love and you can't beat that for perfection

The forties my   favorite decade
age and calendar coincide   common labor 25 cents an hour
dresses of the worst rayon   stockings hideous, heavy, baggy affairs
precious shoe stamp spent on   a silly looking pair
Patriotism a hallowed word   I convinced Herndon he could serve by
raising turkeys and chickens   newspaper work his lifeblood
instead of going to war   he fought slot machines in the paper
his life   was threatened but he said
if a man wants to kill you   he doesn't warn you
he just shoots   he just shoots

When you are forty you know perfection is not necessary
to have a happy marriage and you no longer need to prove it
he made me do the disciplining after telling me what to say
being courteously waited on making a happy home
the greatest of all vocations I wanted everything
to be sweet and attractive without being showy
mine is not an allergy but a lethargy
as dusting is not a creative occupation

Sometimes in church my mind wanders
if a sermon is mediocre I have learned to
worship without listening attend to my meditations
It's time we learned that steering international affairs by
seeing which side can kill the greatest numbers
does not belong here in an enlightened age

My grandchildren's generation have an extra piece that
does not fit call it "Democrat" or what you will
all we can hope is that because they are thinkers
it will be a bonus and something great will come of
their unrecognized pieces their minds
will lead the world to peace, to love and a good moral code
Love, such a simple doctrine so completely comprehensive

We did things we couldn't afford but never did anything we couldn't pay for
our daughter was beautifully behaved in any public place
She was fed at regular hours and punished in a reasonable way. I wished
I could let something go unnoticed Mother said to fight or scratch but
never suffer in silence I was never able to talk about
real sorrow or deep disappointment the times when memories leave scars
I prefer not to discuss them, have
the sea as my therapy. Perhaps it
its very restlessness drains all my tensions and weariness
laps them in to its continual wash.

We Were Taken That Way

We were taken that way at a young age —
the scent of pinesap, a blaze of autumn maples,
fireflies we could catch if we made a tender pocket
with our hands, a rock to climb and a pond for
science where tadpoles fed on algae, changed
overnight into frogs. Pine Mountain's magic.

It was there our grandfather taught us to fish.
First, he made us gather bait, learn
how worms will churn through dirt
so the earth can drain and breathe,
how their leavings continue to feed what is
green, and sometimes they're taken for food.

With the patience of a spider, he taught us
what we needed to know of his mountain —
how to spot poison ivy before grabbing a branch,
how to tell pit vipers from harmless snakes by the slant
of their pupils, and people who openly offered
candy from the few who might use it to seduce.

We wondered why Pa's Smith-Corona sang all night
on the kitchen table, its rhythmic snaps and pings
our lullaby, until he escorted us into *The Pineville Sun*
— his awards and framed letters adorning the walls,
typesetters minding their p's and q's, presses rolling,
their cavernous clatter, the stink of oily ink.

Lately I've uncovered a treasure trove,
solid and precious as pearls suspended in
brine, or maybe more like a snake
discovered beneath a cobwebbed bed,
not knowing if its fangs can force poison
until you can see the shape of its eye.

It's a mission of rescue and search
for fierce truths, buried in an avalanche
of papers he saved for future generations.
Only time will tell, he wrote, hoping
time would redeem him.
Ripples flow from stones thrown long ago.

I wonder what our grandpa would say
Now that his mountain's been scalped
Now that the streams we once sipped
run sick from the spoils,
and brook trout we courted are gone.
It's nothing he could have imagined.

How would he see those *sinister monsters*,
the twists of truth he told to keep them
at bay? Forty years too late to ask him
but not too late for me to recalibrate,
to shade the paint on his portrait,
and let him be.

Tonight our grandfather rests
at my bedside, a half-familiar clone.
I will carry him back over that mountain
where the same current pushes,
and no harm comes
from becoming myself.

Three Colors We Keep Painting: Portraits of
Black Mountain, Kentucky 1931

(after *The Colors She Keeps Painting* by Ellery Akers)

...every resource must be thrown into the battle to drive this insidious monster from our country. Whether Pineville and the Southeastern Kentucky coalfields have followed the right policy in handling the sinister monster that has reared its head in our otherwise peaceful community only time will tell. – Herndon J. Evans, Editor, Pineville Sun

Black for the days, for the mountain
Red for her creeks, blood on her black
Bituminous beds. Black for the gold
Black for the Company's cold ledger line
Black for the hole, the tunnel, the shaft
For each soot-caked face that rose up
From the mine, and the grime that

Turned their bathwater black.
Yellow for teeth. Red for the kisses
On black cracked hands. Black for
Lungs and coughs in the night. Paint
Yellow the God who was treated as
Human. Black for the men who were not
Yellow their scars. Red for the flames
Black the cross left charred in a yard

Black for the shack, the scrip, the kettle
Yellow the gravy and red the beans
Yellow for corn mash steamed in a still
Red the hand caught stealing
For a baby barely breathing
Black for the snake dangling over its bed
Black for the scripture, the prayers
Tiny coffins with hand-painted names

Black for the blast, a wall collapsed
Paint yellow the silenced canary
Black for the railcar, its shadows and tracks
When check-weigh-men's tallies went red

And black soot stuck in every man's nose
Plugs in everyone's ears, yet all were called
Courageous. Red for the strike and the wages
Black for the rifle, the powder and barrel
A deputy's pupil lined in its sight

Black for eviction. Black for the list
Red for all brave empty stomachs
Yellow the eyes searching for rations
Black for the Red Cross agenda —
No work, No eat. Red for the shame
Use black for the pride in
Picket lines where men were named
Yellow for crossing, or signing a
Yellow-dog deal. Fixed were divisions
Between the sides, sharp the myriad slurs

All hope went black with shutting of mines
Failure of union support. Then Red grew
The threat. Paint red for the menace and
Red for the groups — the writers, the students
The ACLU. Red for their pamphlets, their
Rallies, their soup. Black for the
Dynamite blast. Yellow for books with some
Outdated laws. Red for the herrings
Red for the traps. Black the bars of a jail

Black for the state line never to cross and
Cars of the town's vigilantes. Paint yellow
Their high beam headlights in fog, then
Black for the tire iron. Black for the eye
Red for the last fractured nose.
Yellow the cast on hands vindicated —
The braggarts, the badges, the bench

Yellow for twists in reporting the news
For lies and their denials, for claims all
Means were justified, though ends suspend
Unanswered. Blacken the days that remain
Black for the mountain top
Gone with a blast. Black the machines that
Poison the streams where blood spilled red.

Not What You Call Him

I remember the pond,
the bullfrogs, the snakes,
and grandfather's massive hands,
his garden of roses where colors of
crimson and chrome strutted in summer
like the leaves that came screaming
in their autumn mountain reds.

Hands that cradled his garden shears,
pounded typewriter keys to a finish,
sharpened the blades of tools —
slick, honed, and polished
like the words he made
to save his town and its people from
the *slimy serpent, insidious monster,*
the *Reds.*

His were the hands of a crafter —
articulate, agile, assured as the words
that served as poisoned weapons,
loaded, pointed, and charged
to fight with all he had,
no matter what distortions, no matter
that his own hands could turn
a different kind of red.

In times of desperation and terror
slurs are slung over shoulders
like husks and rinds, while claims of
courage, valor, and spinelessness
line up on every side. Some called him
a miserable poltroon, craven coward,
a scoundrel, hired liar, and his
Pineville Sun a *slimy rat sheet.*

Others called him a hero, a sage,
a savior who braved the onslaught
of critics, outsiders and radical ideas,
a protector of democracy,
church, and family.
I remember his mountain.
I gathered his roses, held his hand.
I just called him *Pa*.

Forged in the Glass of a Rearview Mirror

Life can only be understood backwards; but it must be lived forwards
— Soren Kierkegaard

Before I ever combed my hair, I watched
Mom at the mirror as she "did her face"
powder, lipstick, eyeliner, shade —
observed how a woman took care,
before I learned to "do" my own.
Before rejecting the falsity. And that was
before I could appreciate her kind of beauty.

Often I mocked the exaggerations,
scorned her repetitions like
You be accurate, and I'll be attractive
before I knew it was possible to be both.
Then years escaped before her fears
were exposed and I could offer comfort.

My full name was spoken at home
only when I was in trouble, so I tried
to find my distance, before growing to love
the very sound of it, before I laid my claim,
much later to understand the meaning
of carrying our mother's mother's name.

Sometimes you have to live with the weight
of discarding monogrammed handkerchiefs
and pillowslips, engraved silver julep cups,
boxes and boxes of costume jewelry
and dyed satin shoes
before you take in their significance.

It was proper shoes and
pretty things she wanted
as much for me as for herself
and I wanted them too
before I couldn't be bothered,
ran barefoot to college, insisting
how different we were.
Long before I could see
how alike we've become.

What Goes On

Faith

tiny urchin
clings to its rock
spiked spines aimed
at any unwary predator
and nightly feeds on algae
while surges and currents
slowly erode its home

Beach-combing with Mary

A curve of white fluff
surrounded by pieces of bird
called to her
on a sun-drenched beach —
wild flight finished in a flash,
body rendered,
life surrendered to the victor.

Palm cradling the feather-weight,
her outstretched arm arced in tai-chi,
she studied the form, sniffed its edges,
then tasting the scent of babies, she
flashed back decades, disappeared

into awe. I saw death, predator,
prey, and turned away
from the carnage
but not from her, there
in her trance, her dance
that curves toward truth.

I write to begin the day

(after I eat breakfast to begin the day by Zubair Ahmed)

I used to think
I could create time
I was wrong
time creates me
my rituals set a rhythm
that has no rhythm
my rituals begin
with a hand barely moving
warmed by a coffee mug
marks on a page
a hand moves but I don't notice
how the words fall together
black and not black
spaces to hold emotion
I create things
like my breakfast
of berries and yogurt
matter that doesn't matter
words that do
loop and unloop
as destiny unfolds at my table
I will not surrender to clocks
I write to begin the day

Labor Days

I want to dream a fitting phrase
I want to fly
into a bowl full
of refrigeratormagnetwords
and watch them land

Neat and new
in pages
of poignant meanings

But birth means mess
and moments of
agony, contraction,
push and sweat

And yet
the miracle often happens
when we just let go.

Springboard

Today I could only attend
to the clench of my jaw, the
ruffle in my feathers as I wielded
the gardenhose, my weapon
to defend the eaves and beams
from bird leavings.

Next time maybe I'll see
how the barn swallow dives —
double twists, sharp darts,
Ws and Vs penciled on the sky,
wings pulled back to a point,
open, deep beating, then closed,
his quest in bursts and circles
for a ledge to build
a single cup of mud.

This morning while cursing
more thistles and horsetails
for their wicked persistence,
intent on my futile extractions
and what to have for lunch,
the show did go on.

Next time I might notice
how the fiddlehead unfurls
spring coiled, then released
like the flight of a diver —
tuck, pike, half-twist, and free.
Maybe I'll linger long enough
for the fronds to untwist
through time-lapsed frames
into their final swandive pose.

Lan Su Chinese Garden, spring afternoon

The true mystery of the world is the visible, not the invisible
— Oscar Wilde

Through the moon window
in a stuccoed wall
you can see a garden greening,
the arc of a weeping Katsura,
its leaves, pure hearts,
pulse in a faint breeze —
the picture enhanced
by the frame.

A brief rain.
Here are reminders
that downspouts and gutters
silence the music of splash and drip,
that shoes disguise the truth
of wetness.

Tumbled stones misted in drizzle
reveal patterns once planned,
every imperfection splendent.
As light wanes,
opal into indigo,

an orb-weaver completes
her web. Silk tensed
from roof to rail,
she ties one final
sticky strand,
devours three center spirals,
then rests,
waiting for a vibration.

Why Art?

Salmon must swim upstream
not only to spawn and die
but to leave behind
key nutrients
the others
will need
to begin
again.

The artist must make art
to embellish the world,
to expel the dust
of daily life, say
it slant, take us
away to find
and lose
ourselves
to begin
again.

Open a Book of *Night Sounds*
after sculpture by Morse Clary

flutter the pages of
nocturnal rituals
unfurling one
gilded wire inside
a lyre of forest tongues
fine-tuned and plumb
to nothing
but the quiver
of unexpected visitors
yawning into this
small eternity

wing-vested creatures
emerge from the void
where vespers are
whispered and voices
insistent or shrill
ripple through ruffles
of invisible feathers
and one quick wind
rustles the rushes
rattles cicadas' timbals

then silence

not an ending
not a quieting
not an afterthought
this neverstillness

I took my poem to the cemetery

to read to my father. That same warm
wind as the day we buried him
scattered my papers over his grave.
I rearranged the pages, then cleaned
peat and bird stains from the cold
stone bench he had placed there
in the shade of a southern magnolia so
he could sit for a spell next to my mother
those last twelve years without her.

I don't know what I was needing or
how long I stayed. To measure what
can't be measured takes a lifetime of trying.
It was spring, and these words kept repeating
*There is nothing beautiful here. There is nothing
beautiful here.*
But sometimes sorrow soothes,
and there were dogwoods in bloom,
the clean-cut grass, and the hum
of a lawnmower approaching —
the perfect percussion for a poem.

I thought of the man cutting the grass,
how he navigates gravestones, ghosts, and
the living who keep on arriving
in their long black cars, black coats, black
shoes disturbing the mossgreen earth
and his mission to finish before dark,
wondering if he appreciates the peace
in this place with death so close,
and few who would notice his art.

All I wanted for certain that day was to
share a few inspired lines with my Dad,
and maybe Mom too
would overhear my poetry-in-progress
above the background chorus
of mower, birdsong and prayer,
delivered under magnolia's canopy,
from that limestone bench, the only
thing left that could absorb my words,
forever unfinished and complete.

A Visit with the Alchemist

Outside, the sign
reads *We Buy Gold.*
Inside, my hands
clutch silk, felt, and plastic
bags brimming
with bracelets, rings, pins,
spoons, coins, necklaces —
a medley of heritage,
history, and hope.
I take a number and sit
with my mix of suspense,
sorrow and shame,
stirred with glee and sleaze,
and others just like me,
clasping our aspirations
and metals someone
once deemed precious.

A gentle voice
calls *Number Eight.*
With eyes and feet
fixed on the floor,
I deposit a glittering mass
on the glass.
I watch the man's hands
move with a confidence
I cannot share.
He sorts the pieces into piles,
gives some the acid test,
pushes others away,
places a mound on the scale,
strikes a calculator, then
scribbles digits
on a yellow sheet.

I couldn't trace his face
or name his age.
I am focused on numbers and
my mother's gold bracelet —
its charms, my father's gifts.
They toasted trips to foreign lands,
celebrated the arrival of each child,
their five *zero* anniversaries,
and her birthday...
a 14 carat calendar of May,
the fifteenth day filled
with a diamond chip.
These trinkets, her treasures.
How long since
we measured those pleasures
by the dose of her tears?

The man is talking
of weather. He asks where I live,
but I can't hear words.
I can only catch the clink of rings,
beautiful bands, artist-designed,
polished
with vows and promises,
tarnished
by the broken ones.
He weighs their worth,
decides their fate,
makes way for the melt
and meld. And after returning
to their original state,
they will be remade,
infused with newer meanings.
They'll tell another's story,
then again be left behind.

He hands me a check,
moves on to number nine.

Kkoktu *

after sculpture by Byungjoo Suh

The dead don't ask for much —
a grain of rice, a sip of soup, a few gold coins
to appease the messengers,
perhaps a seven-layered shroud,
powder-down blankets and pillows
to soften the bed, a troupe of dancing pallbearers
to spin and toss the casket, then lower it down
with music and a choreographed dance.
A village of figurines might embellish the bier,
give consolation, company, protection
in the journey to beyond.
I would choose the kkoktu doing handstands
to ease my confusion,
and I'd ask him to stay and entertain me
so I might laugh a little longer
at the life I left behind.

While it might be nice to know
there'd be a nicho propped on an altar,
filled with beach stones, a poem, my
favorite jade bracelet and chocolates, or
my placemat and bowl on a table somewhere,
perhaps a phone booth in the wind so
we could carry on our conversations,
I'll settle with ashes absorbed into moss
and a couple of stories
tucked in someone's pocket.

*Kkoktu: Korean funerary figures that come in a procession comprised of a leading Guardian figure, followed by a Caregiver and an Entertainer. In Korean mythology, the dead were believed to be in angst and confusion. To ease the experience of the afterlife, the figures would accompany them to guide, protect, care for, and entertain them.

Layers in the Litter

i.

Touch
fallen feathers long forgotten by the owl,
river-tumbled stones, one finger of a bat wing,
mound of silver lichen cuddled with twigs,
honeycombed bone of antler shed from
its pedicle, just after the velvet withered.
Remember
the times you carried my pack,
helped me cross rushing streams on a log.

ii.

Surely you know that I, too, have cursed
the young buck that rubbed on rosemary shrubs,
because they were mine, and I had plans.
And I have scorned the bat in my rafters
because I felt fear, though I didn't know why.
Yet I have welcomed the echoes of owls,
as if they were given to expand us,
and I never believed a tree would notice
its missing pieces, never knew that my boots
would matter to the lichen-covered rock.

iii.

Yes, I have swallowed more well- polished lies,
now stones in my throat, and I have come to love
a store of things that looked like ours for the taking.
How hard to unravel the passed-down lines
twisted into every sinew and synapse. How hard
to envision this planet where the ones who are gone
are the ones who were gifted with minds
that could plan and imagine, outlasted
by those who could not speak
their poetry in words.

iv.

Listen
as trees carry on their conversations
in silence . If we leave it, the lichen will last,
turning stone into soil so something else
might grow. Bats will adapt as they have
for millions of years. Owls will still fly
with missing feathers. Antlers will thicken,
branch, then shed again. What is lost
will be forgotten, while all that remain
will go on making more of themselves
for as long as they can.

v.

Some time before our final apologies
when we are no longer lulled into believing
that we can own the future, let grief
become our lullaby, and hope
be redefined. May we prolong peace,
if not our species, and not forget the layers left
lying in the litter. There is poetry hidden there
— the music of water over stones, the patterns
in a feather, the warmth in a circle of hands
around the fading fire.

A Change in the Landscape
for John Sangster (1937 - 2013)

I can still feel the soothing,
like a palm on my sternum,
when he'd say *Hello, Elizabeth* —
like it mattered.
the sound of it, the sinking in,
and my slowed breathing.

The quiver in his rich voice —
deep, sincere when reading
pauses as poignant as his phrases,
each fragment vital to the whole.
It seemed as though he knew things
we all could stand to learn
but he didn't know he knew them.

I wanted to say how lucky I was
to watch how he revealed his heart
in humble parts full and hearty —
each clean snapshot a story entire,
the lightness with which he pointed
pathways to living in present tense,
leaning back, or forward, just enough
to return to the fullness.

Strange how his leaving deepened
the learnings.   Sudden,
like a stylus that slid off the record
just when the best part was starting.
Mysterious how lessons sustain.

Left in sway with his island meadows,
now brightened and defined
by autumn's low-moving sun,
now graced by swans returning
as if by defiance of gravity, as if
these fields could remain unchanged.

ACKNOWLEDGEMENTS

My thanks to the editors of the following publications, where these poems, some in slightly different versions, first appeared:

Cirque: One Knee Down in the River
Jabberwock Review: He was the Race Car & I was the Scottie Dog
River Lit: Beach-combing with Mary
The 2River View: Layers in the Litter
3 Elements Review: The Archaeology of Dusting, Learning to Listen, Everyday Delusion
Touch: the Journal of Healing: Everything Changes
Shark Reef: Labor Days
Southern Women's Review: A Visit with the Alchemist

I wish to thank the many who have assisted in bringing this book into the world, and to acknowledge my deep gratitude for:

Val, my life partner, best friend, first reader and chief supporter, who makes all good things in my life possible and whose unwavering love feeds me daily

my Lopez and Orcas Island poet companions who keep poetry and writing alive, worthwhile and fun

the generosity, sensitivity and wise guidance of my poetry friend and advisor, Jill McCabe Johnson

Lynne Keeley's incisive and patient assistance with layout and design

Karen Russell's ideas and instructions on how to change photographs into sketches

my parents and grandparents who, though no longer with us, continue to influence my life

my current family and friends who believe in me, even when I doubt myself, and without whose encouragement, this endeavor would not have been possible

Terry Martin's simple, indelible words, *If you want to write, write!,* that nudged me off the diving board years ago

fellow Lopez Island poet, John Sangster, who inspired me to say "Yes" to poetry

my brother, Baylor, who taught me to say "Yes" to life

About the Author

Elizabeth Evans Landrum grew up in Louisville, Kentucky, and currently resides in her "true home", the Pacific Northwest. She earned a Ph.D. in Clinical Psychology from the University of Louisville, then began a 30 year psychotherapy practice, in Louisville and later, in Edmonds, Washington.

She lives with her wife and dog on Lopez Island in the Salish Sea where she enjoys retirement time for writing, creating journals and cards, and volunteering. Her poems have appeared in numerous print and on-line journals. *Shelf Life* is her first published collection.

CPSIA information can be obtained
at www.ICGtesting.com
Printed in the USA
FSHW010324040619
58698FS